BIRD'S EYE VIEW
THE NATURAL WORLD

JOHN FARNDON   **PAUL BOSTON**

words & pictures

Quarto is the authority on a wide range of topics.
Quarto educates, entertains and enriches the lives of our readers—enthusiasts and lovers of hands-on living.
www.quartoknows.com

© 2019 Quarto Publishing plc
Text © John Farndon
Illustrations © Paul Boston

John Farndon has asserted his right to be identified as the author of this work.
Paul Boston has asserted his right to be identified as the illustrator of this work.

First published in 2019 by words & pictures, an imprint of The Quarto Group.
6 Orchard Road, Suite 100, Lake Forest, CA 92630.
T: +1 949 380 7510
F: +1 949 380 7575
www.quartoknows.com

A CIP record for this book is available from the Library of Congress.

ISBN: 978 1 78603 893 7

9 8 7 6 5 4 3 2 1
Manufactured in Shenzhen, China PP052019

FSC
www.fsc.org
MIX
Paper from responsible sources
FSC® C001701

Climb on board this once-in-a-lifetime balloon journey for a unique view of Planet Earth.

Contents

Flying the World

Hold on tight! We're about to go on an adventure, up into the sky to see the natural world spread out below. As we go on our journey, we'll get a brilliant bird's eye view of its amazing landscapes, and the animals and plants that live in them. Starting in the Florida Everglades, follow our journey across the map below. Ready?

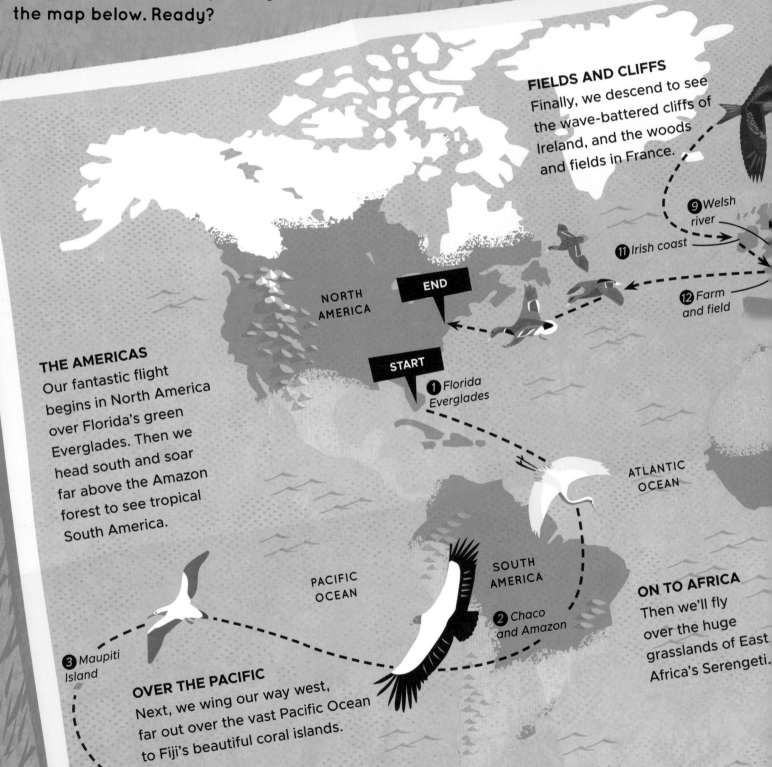

FIELDS AND CLIFFS
Finally, we descend to see the wave-battered cliffs of Ireland, and the woods and fields in France.

NORTH AMERICA

END

START

1 Florida Everglades

9 Welsh river

11 Irish coast

12 Farm and field

THE AMERICAS
Our fantastic flight begins in North America over Florida's green Everglades. Then we head south and soar far above the Amazon forest to see tropical South America.

ATLANTIC OCEAN

PACIFIC OCEAN

SOUTH AMERICA

2 Chaco and Amazon

3 Maupiti Island

OVER THE PACIFIC
Next, we wing our way west, far out over the vast Pacific Ocean to Fiji's beautiful coral islands.

ON TO AFRICA
Then we'll fly over the huge grasslands of East Africa's Serengeti.

ICY REALM
Now off we speed to Europe to see how rivers run, then even farther north into the icy Arctic. Brrr!

ARCTIC OCEAN

⑩ Northern Scandinavia

EUROPE

SEA OF GRASS
Higher and higher, we'll soar—over the vast steppe grasslands of Central Asia.

⑥ Asian steppes

ASIA

PACIFIC OCEAN

⑦ Himalayas

⑤ Guilin Hills

ROCKS AND HILLS
Next, it's on to Uluru rock in Australia's empty heartland before swooping in on China's magical Guilin Hills.

INDIAN OCEAN

⑧ East Africa

TOWERING PEAKS
Then back we'll go over the peaks of the Himalayas, the world's tallest mountain chain.

AFRICA

AUSTRALIA

④ Uluru

SOUTHERN OCEAN

5

Water and Grass

Florida's steamy Everglades is a wet, wet land—not quite a marsh, nor yet a river. Water seeps from Lake Okeechobee through swamps and patches of grass and twists between tree-filled islands called hammocks.

On the hammock islands, rare animals like the Florida panther and Key deer hide safely among tropical oaks and gumbo limbo trees.

Key deer

Florida panther

Great white egret

In the shallows, you might see big birds with long legs such as roseate spoonbills and egrets. They wade in the water and dip their beaks below the surface, searching for shellfish.

Roseate spoonbill

On the coast, tangles of mangrove trees stand in the salty water on stilt-like roots. Manatees swim lazily between the roots, grazing on underwater seagrass.

West Indian manatee

Everglades

Great barracuda

MANGROVE AND KEYS

WATERWAYS AND SLOUGHS

American alligator

West Indian manatee

Roseate spoonbill

Bottlenose dolphin

large area of dark green cypress trees is called "Big
ypress." Cypress trees are conifers like pines, but water
ps around their knobbly roots, which are called "knees."

In clear channels, you may glimpse fish such as
tarpon. But watch out for alligators! They lurk
in "sloughs" where the water clogs up—ready
to snap their jaws on the unwary!

*Everglades
kite*

Alligator

The water winds through tall
swamps of sawgrass—so
called for its sharp, sawlike
edges. Not many animals live
here, but there are "holes"
where alligators nest.

A line of islands or "keys" sits on
a reef that has been built over
thousands of years by tiny corals.
Turtles and dolphins swim in the
seas around them, along with
barracuda and other fish.

Anhinga

*Florida
softshell turtle*

*Bottlenose
dolphin*

HAMMOCKS AND ISLANDS

Key deer

*Eastern indigo
snake*

EVERGLADE BIRDS

da softshell turtle

rpon

Florida panther

Anhinga

Everglades kite

*Great
white
egret*

Every year, torrential rains flood the flatlands in the east to create a marsh as big as Washington state in the US. It is called the Pantanal, and it teems with wildlife.

Great egret

Where Brazil meets Argentina, the Iguazu River plunges over a cliff into a gorge in one of the world's largest waterfalls—a thunderous torrent of white water.

Jabiru stork

Naked-tailed armadillo

Anteater

Hunters roam the grass, from big cats like jaguars and pumas to smaller cats such as ocelots, the pampas cat, and Geoffroy's cat.

HUNTERS

Jaguar

Yacare caiman

There are few hiding places in the open grass from birds of prey, such as vultures. Greater rheas can run so fast, they have no need to fly.

GRASSLAND BIRD

Red-crested cardinal

Greater rhea

There are palm trees dotted amid the grass and clumps of dark, thorny quebracho trees. Look out for termite nests, too. They make good larders for hungry anteaters and armadillos.

King vulture

The Chaco is a mixture of dry tropical forest and grassland that stretches from the lofty Andes in the west to the wild Paraná River in the east. Sometimes, the grass is so tall a rider could hide in it!

Tall, flightless rhea birds are striding through the grass. Herds of gray brocket and pampas deer graze among the tall stems.

South America

PACIFIC OCEAN

ATLANTIC OCEAN

Tropical grassland
With too little rain here for lush forests, there are patches of spiky trees, such as the quebracho. Its wood is so hard, quebracho means "axe-breaker."

Quebracho

There is plenty of grass, so the biggest animals in the Chaco are grazers, such as deer.

Capybara

Gray brocket deer

GRASSLAND MAMMALS

Pampas deer

Flying the Tropics

It's warm all year round in the heart of tropical South America. Yet some places get soaked with rain while others are as dry as deserts. That's why the landscape is so varied—from the dense Amazon forest to the vast Gran Chaco grasslands.

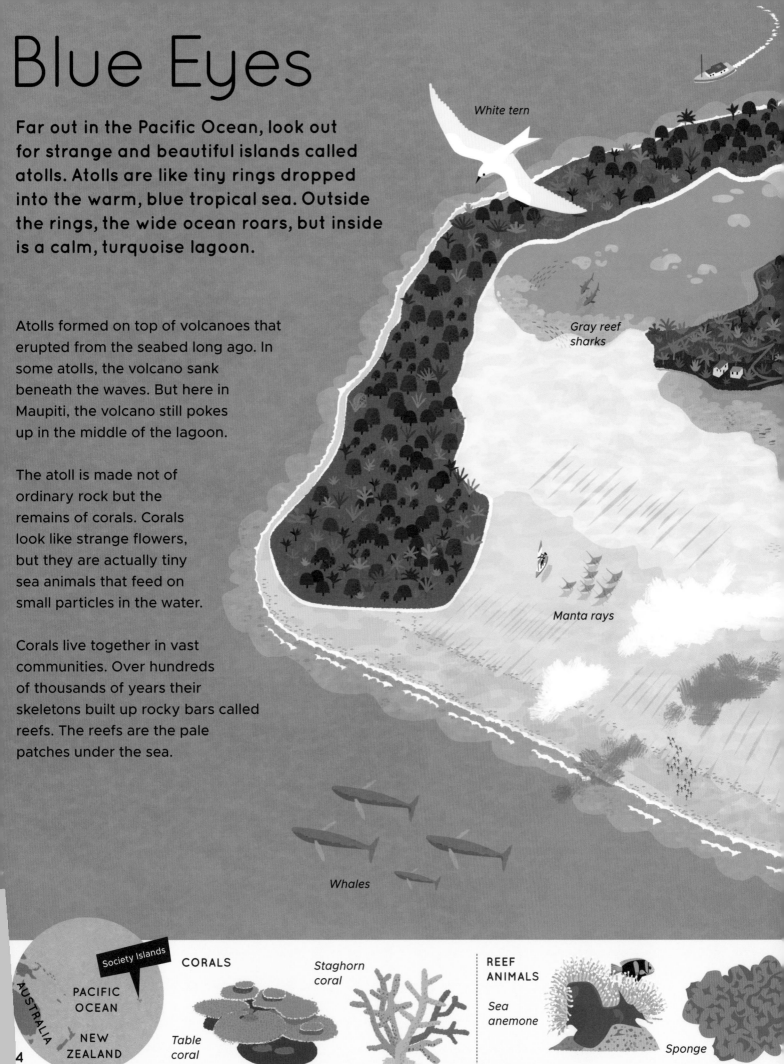

Blue Eyes

Far out in the Pacific Ocean, look out for strange and beautiful islands called atolls. Atolls are like tiny rings dropped into the warm, blue tropical sea. Outside the rings, the wide ocean roars, but inside is a calm, turquoise lagoon.

Atolls formed on top of volcanoes that erupted from the seabed long ago. In some atolls, the volcano sank beneath the waves. But here in Maupiti, the volcano still pokes up in the middle of the lagoon.

The atoll is made not of ordinary rock but the remains of corals. Corals look like strange flowers, but they are actually tiny sea animals that feed on small particles in the water.

Corals live together in vast communities. Over hundreds of thousands of years their skeletons built up rocky bars called reefs. The reefs are the pale patches under the sea.

White tern

Gray reef sharks

Manta rays

Whales

AUSTRALIA

Society Islands

PACIFIC OCEAN

NEW ZEALAND

CORALS

Staghorn coral

Table coral

REEF ANIMALS

Sea anemone

Sponge

4

It's not only warm in the Amazon, it also rains all year round. This is perfect for trees to grow thick, green, and lush. They form the world's largest tropical rainforest.

Many creatures live in the bright treetops of the Amazon rainforest. Some fly there, such as birds and bats, while others climb, like sloths and monkeys.

Egrets and storks wing their way over the rivers. Huge guinea pig-like capybara cool off in river mud. But they need to watch out for hungry predators like giant anacondas and jaguars!

Anaconda

...opical forest
...e lush rainforest
...s a huge variety of
...es. Many trees grow
...l to catch the sun
...d rain. They have
...ry tough wood to
...rry their big leaves.

Brazil nut tree

There's little grass in the forest, but lots of small creatures scurry around, browsing and foraging in the bushy undergrowth.

FOREST MAMMALS

Peccary

Sloth

Spider monkey

It's steamy and shady down on the forest floor. Here, pig-like peccaries browse on the vegetation while countless insects scurry and buzz through the gloom.

Harpy eagle

Beyond the forest where it's drier, trees grow sparse, and the landscape spreads out in a vast grassland called the Cerrado.

The largest hunters in this region are cats, such as jaguars and ocelots, but they have been hunted almost to extinction.

Ocelot

FOREST BIRDS

The rainforest is filled with colorful birds, such as parrots and hoatzins, especially high up in the treetops.

Hummingbird

Scarlet macaw

Tou

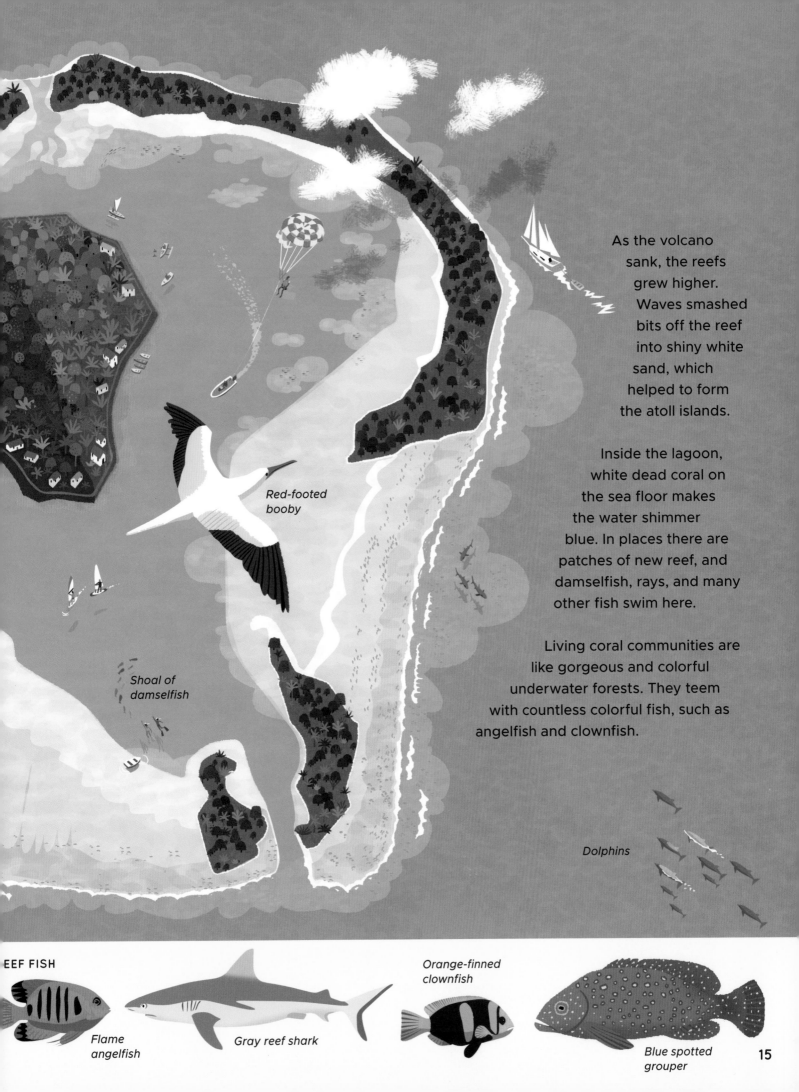

As the volcano sank, the reefs grew higher. Waves smashed bits off the reef into shiny white sand, which helped to form the atoll islands.

Inside the lagoon, white dead coral on the sea floor makes the water shimmer blue. In places there are patches of new reef, and damselfish, rays, and many other fish swim here.

Living coral communities are like gorgeous and colorful underwater forests. They teem with countless colorful fish, such as angelfish and clownfish.

Red-footed booby

Shoal of damselfish

Dolphins

EEF FISH

Flame angelfish

Gray reef shark

Orange-finned clownfish

Blue spotted grouper

Kata Tjuta

The Great Rock

The middle of Australia is vast and very empty desert. Then suddenly, you see a strange giant rock bursting from the sand. This is Uluru, and it is sacred to the ancient peoples of Australia.

Far off to the east of Uluru is another rock formation called Kata Tjuta. This is also sacred to Australia's ancient peoples.

Uluru looks bone dry. But it has rained enough over the ages to wear deep grooves down the rock's sides. Specks of rusty iron in the rock make it glow in the rising sun.

Emu

Perentie

Thorny devil

Brush-tailed mulgara

Around it, clumps of spinifex grass bake in the desert heat. So too do reptiles such as scary looking thorny devils and huge perentie lizards. Even kangaroos and hopping mice may find enough to eat and drink.

Southern marsupial mole

Uluru

AUSTRALIA

ULURU BIRDS

Walawaru —wedge-tailed eagle

Piya piyarpa —galah

Emu

ULURU REPTILES

Tjakura —great desert sk[...]

Ngiyari— thorny devil

Lake Amadeus

Far away to the north is Lake Amadeus. It is usually a dry, shiny patch of salt, but sometimes it fills with water.

Wedge-tailed eagle

Galah

Red kangaroo

Dingo

Uluru is just the tip of a vast slab of tough arkose rock. It was once buried entirely in sand, but has been exposed by millions of years of wind and rain.

Great desert skink

Spinifex hopping mouse

ULURU MAMMALS

Malu—red kangaroo

Southern marsupial mole

Ngintaka—perentie

Papa inura—dingo

Tarkawara—spinifex hopping mouse

Brush-tailed mulgara

Green Peaks

The Guilin Hills in China are not rounded like most other hills. They are an amazing landscape of pointy green peaks with rivers winding through them far below. This beautiful landscape has inspired Chinese painters for a thousand years.

Long ago, there was only sea here. But over time, the shells and bones of sea creatures piled up on top of one another on the ocean floor, eventually turning to solid limestone rock.

Forty million years ago, earthquakes lifted the rock out of the sea to make a vast plateau. Then slowly, mildly acidic rain dissolved the rock to form Guilin's unique peaks.

Temminck's tragopan

Golden pheasant

Pit viper

Chinese pond heron

Chinese giant salamander

Guilin Hills
CHINA

BIRDS OF THE VALLEY

Little egret

Chinese pond heron

Chinese hwamei

REPTILES AND AMPHIBIANS

Schmacker's frog

Chinese giant salamander

Over Woods and Grass

In the winter, the vast center of Asia is icy cold, but as we fly over in the summer, it's pleasantly warm. To the north, enough rain falls to allow woods to grow. Farther south, there's only enough rain for grass and in some places even less rain falls, leaving only dry deserts.

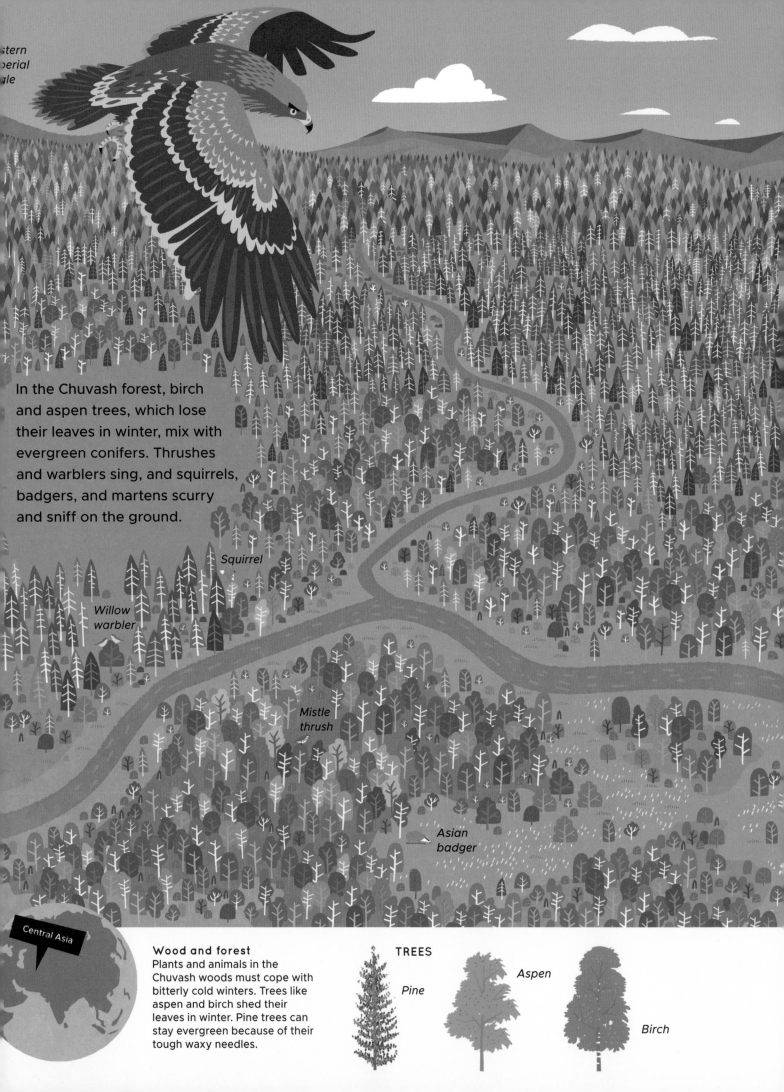

stern
perial
le

In the Chuvash forest, birch and aspen trees, which lose their leaves in winter, mix with evergreen conifers. Thrushes and warblers sing, and squirrels, badgers, and martens scurry and sniff on the ground.

Squirrel

Willow warbler

Mistle thrush

Asian badger

Central Asia

Wood and forest
Plants and animals in the Chuvash woods must cope with bitterly cold winters. Trees like aspen and birch shed their leaves in winter. Pine trees can stay evergreen because of their tough waxy needles.

TREES

Pine

Aspen

Birch

In the distance, you can see the blue haze of the ancient Ural mountains. They are not very high but they run from north to south across the whole of Russia.

Roe deer

Houbara bustard

Beyond the Volga river, the trees thin out into stretches of grass called "forest steppe." Look for the rare Przewalski's horse—it may be the only truly wild horse in the world.

Bobak marmot

WOODLAND ANIMALS

Red squirrel

Asian badger

WOODLAND BIRDS

Willow warbler

Mistle thrush

Forest steppe
Forest steppe occurs where it's too dry in places for trees. But the mix of trees and grass is great for some animals.

Speckled ground squirrel

The lofty pillars of rock are called "fenglin." Clusters of fenglin are called "fengcong." Evergreen oak trees and laurel trees grow on their steep sides, with their roots clinging to the cracks in the rock.

Little egret

Up among the trees, you may see monkeys, or colorful birds such as tragopan and golden pheasants.

Water buffalo

Snub-nosed monkey

Farmers here grow rice in flooded fields called paddies, or raise cows.

People catch fish in the beautiful River Li that winds through the hills. Amazingly, the fishermen train cormorant birds to dive for fish for them.

White-lipped pit viper

BIRDS OF THE HILLS

Golden pheasant

Temminck's tragopan

Silver oriole

ANIMALS OF THE CHINESE HILLS

Water buffalo

Snub-nosed monkey

Giant panda

19

Going Up

We're now flying over the Kali Gandaki gorge in the Himalayas, the world's highest mountains. The slopes are divided into natural zones, rising from warm forests to peaks that are always covered in snow.

Himalayan golden eagle

Yak

Himalayan pika

Snow leopard

Takin

Golden langur monkey

Clouded leopard

Asian elephant

Himalayas

INDIA

ANIMALS OF THE MOUNTAIN FIRS

Red panda

Takin

Alpine musk deer

HIGH-LIVING ANIMALS

Himalayan marmot

Pika

Tahr

Lightning strikes can trigger wildfires in the bone-dry grass.

Demoiselle crane

Saiga antelope

Steppe eagle

There's nowhere to hide in the open steppe. So rodents that live here, like marmots and pikas, burrow into the ground to escape steppe kites and eagles that swoop and swirl above.

Przewalski's horse

At last, there's only a vast sea of grass, rolling away as far as the eye can see. It's called the steppe in Asia, and is like the prairies in North America.

Speckled ground squirrel

Corsac fox

EPPE ANIMALS

Przewalski's horse

Asian houbara bustard

Steppe
At first, the only animals you spot on the steppe are herds of horses and antelope. But look closely, and you will see many rodents and lots of birds.

Bobak marmot

Corsac fox

In the distance sit the glistening skyscrapers of Kazakhstan's capital city.

The dry south of Kazakhstan is a windswept desert of sand dunes and camels. In the middle of the desert is the Baikonur rocket site, where spaceships have been launched for more than 60 years.

Pallid harrier

Bactrian camel

The Aral Sea was once a huge sea, teeming with fish, fed with water by the Syr Darya river. But after the Syr Darya river was diverted to water crops in the 1960s, the Aral shrank dramatically, leaving stranded the rusting remains of many fishing boats.

STEPPE BIRDS

Saiga antelope

Demoiselle crane

Pin-tailed sandgrouse

Steppe eagle

Pallid harrie

Himalayan golden eagle

Bar-headed goose

Red panda

Musk deer

Asian black bear

Tiger

In the distance and beyond the peaks, the windswept and grassy Tibetan plateau stretches far into the distance. This chilly region is home to yak and Tibetan antelope.

Above 14,750 feet (4,500 m), it's as bleak as the Arctic—yet birds, such as rosy pipits and chough, find seeds and insects to eat. Overhead, eagles scan for prey with their sharp eyes.

It's so chilly above 13,000 feet (4,000 m) there's only grass and rocks. Yet hardy little gentian and saxifrage flowers spread patches of color. Pikas and mountain voles scurry here and there.

Only small bushes, such as rhododendron, survive above 9,850 feet (3,000 m). But you can see blue sheep and goatlike tahrs and, if you're lucky, a snow leopard or two!

It's so cool above 6,500 feet (2,000 m) you can only see dark-green conifer trees, such as pine and fir, as well as patches of bamboo. Red pandas, musk deer, and goat-antelopes called takin browse and forage in the gloom.

Up in the cooler foothills, there are oak and maple trees. Golden langur monkeys scamper along their branches, and you might glimpse a black bear or a clouded leopard.

Each year, heavy monsoon rains help thick tropical forests to grow on the plain. These forests are home to elephants, tigers, and birds, although many of these trees are cleared for farms.

Wild yak

HIGH-FLYING BIRDS

Alpine chough

Himalayan griffon

HIGH FLOWERS

Saxifrage

Rhododendron

Himalayan balsam

The Great Trek

Every spring in East Africa it stops raining and the grassy plains dry out. Can you see the vast herds of hungry wildebeest—snorting, bucking, and kicking up dust? They are taking part in a long circular journey to find fresh grass, joined by zebras and gazelles.

Baboon

4 Eventually, the skies will darken, rain will fall, and the animals will head off south again to catch the new grass. On their way, males and females mate and the herds cross rivers full of crocodiles again.

Red-billed quelea

Turacos

3 By August, the rivers will be entirely dry. But by then the weary wildebeest are in the greener woodlands of the northwest where they linger for a while, grazing in the shade.

Serengeti

GRAZERS

Plains zebra

White-bearded wildebeest

Thomson's gazelle

Hippopotamus

BROWSERS
Giraffe

5 By the year end, the wildebeest will be back on the high plains in the southeast of the Serengeti where they started. The grass is fresh, and calves are born. They can stay a while.

1 The herd's journey began at the start of May when the grass died on the high plains. The animals moved off, with zebra leading the way, followed by wildebeest, and finally gazelles. On the trek, they were hunted by lions and hunting dogs.

Rüppell's vulture

Gazelle

Giraffe

Lion

Hunting dog

Ostrich

2 The herd leaders now face the wild Grumeti river, but the water is full of snapping crocodiles! There is a lot of pushing from behind, so the animals plunge in and swim for their lives. Not all of them will make it.

Zebra

Black rhinoceros

HUNTERS

Cheetah

Lion

Hunting dog

Spotted hyena

SCAVENGERS

Olive baboon

Rüppell's vulture

PICKERS

Ostrich

Going Down

From high above you can see a river's entire course. It starts as a trickle high in the Welsh hills, then flows right down to the sea, getting ever bigger as other streams join it.

The river begins as a little stream tumbling over rocks and waterfalls. Salmon swim up here from the sea each year to lay eggs in pools. Dippers bob in and out of the water looking for insect larvae and tiny fish.

Farther down, the stream becomes a smooth flowing river and winds through a woody valley. Otters plop into the water and kingfishers wait on branches to look for fish.

Heron

Otter

River Usk

MOUNTAIN BIRDS

Red kite

White-throated dipper

Common sandpiper

MOUNTAIN STREAM FISH

Atlantic salmon

Beyond the valley, the river is deep and wide. It bends over the plain in big loops, called meanders, and it often floods. Along the banks, holes among the willow tree roots make homes for water voles.

In wet marshes, tall birds called herons stand in the water waiting for fish. But, with their sharp teeth, big fish called pike can be more than a match for herons.

At last, the river reaches the sea through a broad estuary. When the sea tide goes out, it may uncover vast stretches of soggy mud called mudflats.

Red kite

Gray wagtail

Salmon

Dipper

Bullhead

Minnow

ON THE MIDDLE RIVER

Eurasian otter

Common kingfisher

ON THE WIDE RIVER

Trout

Pike

Gray heron

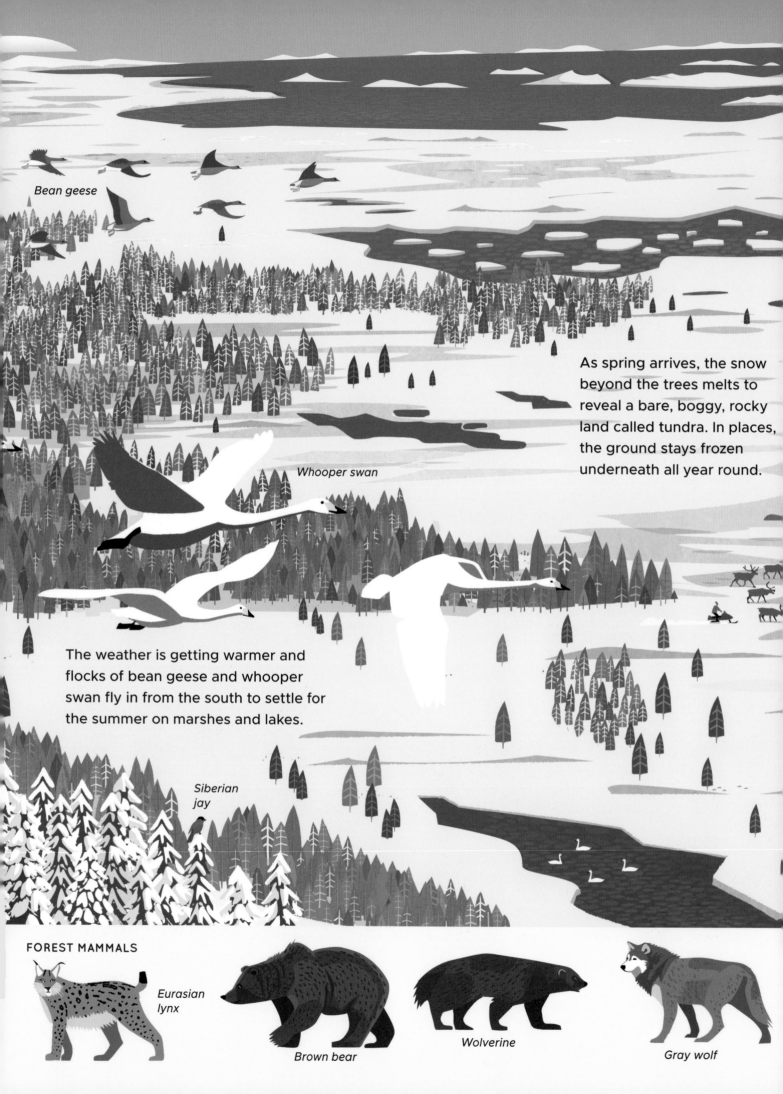

Bean geese

Whooper swan

As spring arrives, the snow beyond the trees melts to reveal a bare, boggy, rocky land called tundra. In places, the ground stays frozen underneath all year round.

The weather is getting warmer and flocks of bean geese and whooper swan fly in from the south to settle for the summer on marshes and lakes.

Siberian jay

FOREST MAMMALS

Eurasian lynx

Brown bear

Wolverine

Gray wolf

Under the snow, the waxy needles of the conifer trees stayed green. So the taiga forest continued to give animals food and shelter throughout the winter.

Northern hawk-owl

During the winter months, little rodents kept warm in burrows, eating seeds and berries—or were dinner for the fierce wolverine and lynx cat! Brown bears were in a long winter sleep, called a torpor.

Siberian tits and jays flit among the branches. Grouse rummage on the ground for needles and berries, while a deadly hawk owl hunts above for voles.

Gray wolf

Brown bear

Eurasian lynx

Eurasian black grouse

Wolverine

Scandinavia

Boreal forest
The bitter conifer needles of the northern forest are tough for animals to live on. But the trees shelter creatures that can brave it out though the winter from the worst of the cold.

FOREST BIRDS

Northern hawk-owl

Eurasian black grouse

Siberian jay

Arctic Flight

The long, cold winter of northern Scandinavia is almost over. In the vast dark conifer forests, or taiga, to the south, snow is sliding off the branches. In the bleak tundra farther north, you can already see patches of green.

Far across the icy sea on Svalbard island, there are polar bears. But the bears are in danger. They need sea ice to move around. But as the world's climate warms, a lot of ice has melted.

Orca

Polar be

Harp seal

Out at sea, the winter ice is breaking up. Seals slip between cracks, often chased by orcas. Eider ducks prepare to leave their winter homes in the fjords, or inlets.

Common eider duck

Snow bunting

Rock ptarmigan

Eider duck

Arctic
For half the year it is almost pitch black in the Arctic. Yet a few animals stay all year, and there is abundant life in the sea.

ANIMALS OF THE ICY SEA

Harp seal

Polar bear

Orca (killer whale)

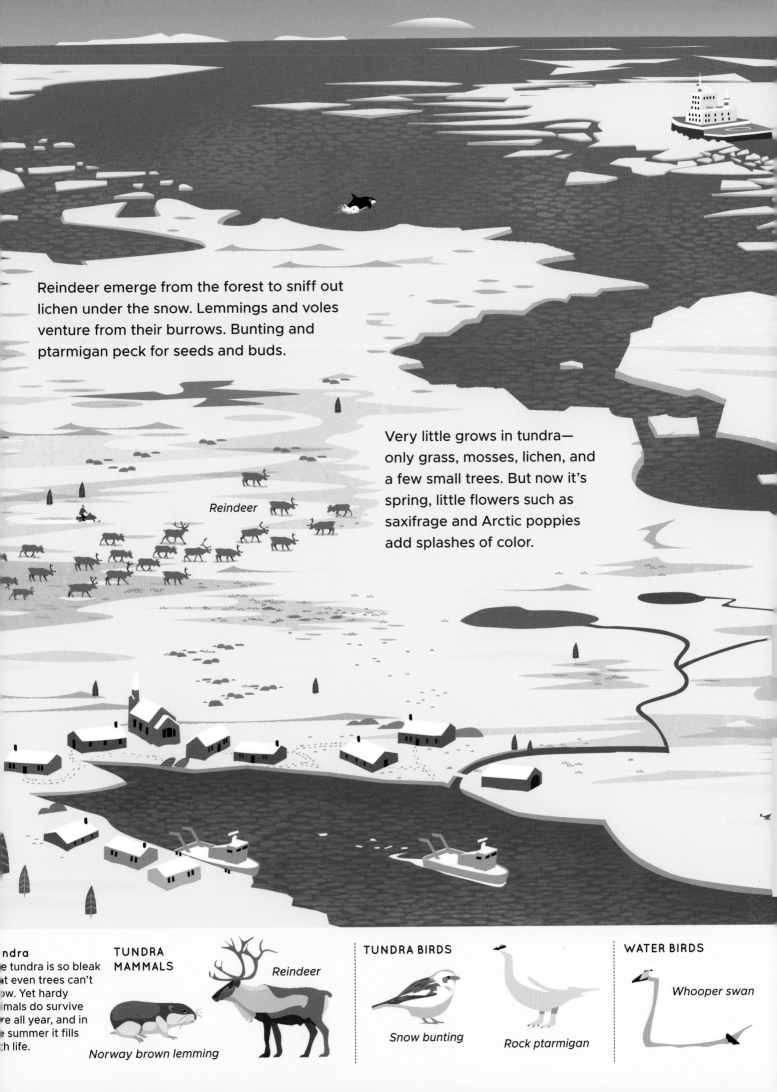

Reindeer emerge from the forest to sniff out lichen under the snow. Lemmings and voles venture from their burrows. Bunting and ptarmigan peck for seeds and buds.

Reindeer

Very little grows in tundra— only grass, mosses, lichen, and a few small trees. But now it's spring, little flowers such as saxifrage and Arctic poppies add splashes of color.

ndra
e tundra is so bleak
t even trees can't
w. Yet hardy
mals do survive
re all year, and in
e summer it fills
h life.

TUNDRA MAMMALS

Reindeer

Norway brown lemming

TUNDRA BIRDS

Snow bunting

Rock ptarmigan

WATER BIRDS

Whooper swan

Shore Thing

Now we're soaring over Ireland's west coast, where it meets the wild Atlantic Ocean. On some coasts, waves lap gently on beaches, but here, mountainous waves crash against rocks to carve out the towering Cliffs of Moher.

Sea birds nest on the cliff out of reach of hunting animals. You can see huge flocks of gulls, guillemots, fulmars, and kittiwakes, and puffins scurrying into burrows on the cliff top.

Atlantic puffin

Kittiwake

Fulmar

Guillemot

At the foot of the cliff, the crashing waves have carved out a platform in the rock. Twice a day, when the tide goes out, it leaves little rock pools behind.

Limpets and mussels cling fast to exposed rocks. Rock pools are natural aquariums, where crabs and anemones tuck themselves away until the tide washes in again.

Hermit crab

Gray seal

Bladder wrack seaweed

In the shelter between headlands, sand smashed from the cliffs may wash up to form a beach. Line seaweed on the beach show where the tide reach

Cliffs of Moher

ATLANTIC OCEAN

CLIFF BIRDS

Herring gull

Kittiwake

Atlantic puffin

SHORE DWELLERS

Hermit crab

Anemone

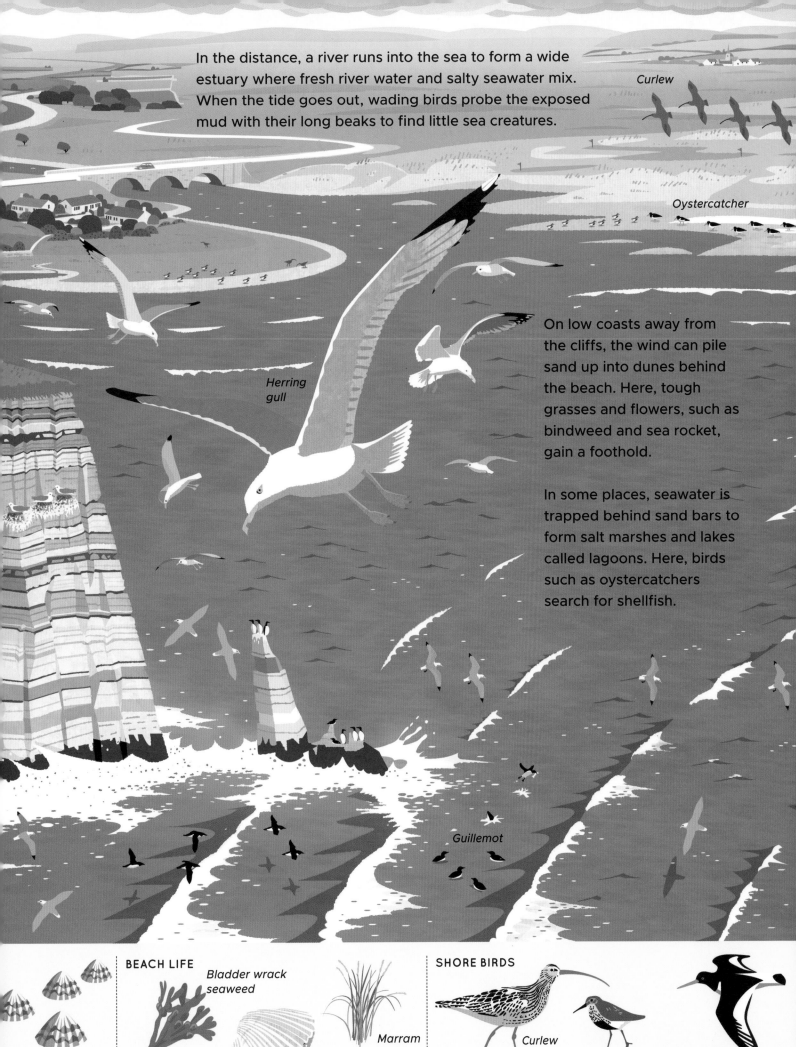

In the distance, a river runs into the sea to form a wide estuary where fresh river water and salty seawater mix. When the tide goes out, wading birds probe the exposed mud with their long beaks to find little sea creatures.

Curlew

Oystercatcher

Herring gull

On low coasts away from the cliffs, the wind can pile sand up into dunes behind the beach. Here, tough grasses and flowers, such as bindweed and sea rocket, gain a foothold.

In some places, seawater is trapped behind sand bars to form salt marshes and lakes called lagoons. Here, birds such as oystercatchers search for shellfish.

Guillemot

Limpet

BEACH LIFE

Bladder wrack seaweed

Scallop

Marram grass

SHORE BIRDS

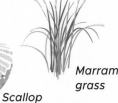

Curlew

Dunlin

Oystercatcher

39

Field and Forest

Don't the fields and forest look green and natural spread out below? But the French countryside is only partly natural. It has been shaped mostly by farmers over the ages, and has its own special blend of wildlife.

People changed old woods by collecting firewood and chopping down trees for timber. Yet deer, badgers, squirrels, and dormice make homes here. In spring, bluebells and other flowers spread a carpet under the trees.

Long-eared bat

Many forests have been cut down entirely to make fields. The cows are grazing in pastures where there was once only trees.

Roe deer

Where people cleared trees in the woods, stag beetles burrow in tree stumps and woodpeckers tap their beaks on trees to get at insects inside. Bats hide here too, sleeping in old trees during the day.

Green woodpecker

Badger

Boar

Harvest mouse

Normandy, France

ANIMALS OF THE HEDGEROW

Long-eared bat

Hedgehog

Beech marten

FIELD FLOWERS

Marigold

Cornflo

Over in the old farm buildings, you might see bats, house martins, starlings, and sparrows, and even a barn owl.

Starlings

Skylark

House martin

This empty field is a meadow. The cows have been moved out to allow grass to grow into hay to be cut for animal feed later in the year. Now the meadow is filled with buttercups and daisies.

Barn owl

Hedgehog

Fields plowed to grow wheat and barley are tough places for animals. Yet you might glimpse hares, moles, harvest mice, and field voles here, or hear a skylark soaring into the air, singing.

Partridge

Beech marten

The old hedgerows that separate some fields are made of tangles of hawthorn and honeysuckle. They are not just barriers, but provide homes for hedgehogs, bank voles, and dormice.

Hare

Red squirrel

Poppy

FIELD BIRDS

Corn bunting

Red-legged partridge

Starling

FIELD ANIMALS

Field mouse

Hare

Field vole

41

Down to Earth

Watch out for the bump—we're coming into land! We've just flown all the way around the world. We've gazed down on everything from polar bears in the Arctic to kangaroos in Australia. What an amazing world of nature we live in, and that's just the beginning.

It's an amazing view, but it's also very fragile. Developing the human world by building farms and cities and producing endless new products and waste changes the world. Did you spot on our flight some of the damage humans can do—cutting down trees in the Amazon, copper waste from Karabash in the Urals, and oil pollution in the Arctic ocean?

The landscapes we've seen here are shrinking fast, and with them many wild animals are being lost forever. Yet there's still hope. Nature continues to thrive, even close to home. Look carefully and discover the natural world all around you.